IT IS
FINISHED

Seven Sayings from the Cross

J.JOHN

Ⓟ PHILO TRUST

First published in 2015 by Philo Trust,
Witton House, Lower Road, Chorleywood, Rickmansworth, WD3 5LB, United Kingdom

Reprinted in 2016

www.canonjjohn.com

British Library Cataloguing in Publication Data

A catalogue record for this book is available from the British Library

ISBN: 978-0-9928399-7-0

Photos by: NBC/NBCU Photo Bank via Getty Images

Design by Simon Parry and Verité

Print Management by Verité CM Ltd
www.veritecm.com

IT IS
FINISHED

Seven Sayings from the Cross

J.JOHN

Father, forgive them,
for they do not know
what they are doing

(Luke 23:34)

ONE

There are many ways of thinking about Easter. One with a long tradition is to consider what Jesus said while he was on the cross. The four Gospel writers record seven sayings (traditionally called the 'Seven Last Words') spoken by Jesus on the cross, which overflow with meaning. Taken together they sum up what Easter – and Christianity – means.

The background is that some time in the morning of the first Good Friday, immediately after the evening that saw the start of the feast of the Passover, Jesus was nailed to the cross. The Gospel writers record that, as Jesus hung on the cross, from noon to three in the afternoon an unexplained darkness fell upon the earth. It is a darkness that echoes what Christ experienced: a death somehow worse than death.

Here, in the first of the seven sayings, Jesus offers up a prayer for his persecutors: 'Father, forgive them, for they do not know what they are doing.' In view of what Jesus says later on, it is important to notice that here he refers to God as 'Father' or, in the original Aramaic, '*Abba*'. This was the normal way that Jesus prayed to God, showing how he knew God in a personal way.

The really important thing here is the way that Jesus prays for others. It is a remarkable prayer. Most of us have problems praying for good people at good times. What is remarkable here is that Jesus is able to pray for bad people at a bad time. Here, in this desperate situation and in appalling pain, Jesus' concern remains for others. In praying like this, he is living out his own teaching: 'But to you who are listening I say: love your enemies, do good to those who hate you, bless those who curse you, pray for those who ill-treat you' (Luke 6:27–28). Jesus is that extraordinary rarity in human history: a moral teacher who lives out what he says.

Notice, too, the content of the prayer; Jesus pleads, 'Forgive them, for they do not know what they are doing.' Jesus puts forward what we might call in legal language 'extenuating circumstances' – the fact that his persecutors didn't fully realise that they were mocking and torturing the Messiah, the Son of God.

In his first letter, the apostle John writes, 'My dear children, I write this to you so that you will not sin. But if anybody does sin, we have an advocate with the Father – Jesus Christ, the Righteous One' (1 John 2:1). St John uses a legal term (παράκλητον) to describe the role of Jesus, a word we might translate as 'defence lawyer'. What this word actually means in practice is shown perfectly on the cross.

Jesus asks his heavenly Father to forgive people and offers every possible excuse for them. That's what we all need, even the best of us: a God who, in Jesus, is on our side and who speaks on our behalf.

Ponder: *Who then will condemn us? No one – for Christ Jesus died for us and was raised to life for us, and he is sitting in the place of honour at God's right hand, pleading for us.*

Romans 8:34, NLT

Prayer: Thank you, Lord God, that you are on our side. Give us the capacity to forgive others as you have forgiven us. Amen.

Truly I tell you, today you will be with me in paradise

(Luke 23:43)

TWO

It is a universal feature of human societies that there are hierarchies. There are always those at the top who are successes, and at the bottom those who have failed. One of the humiliations poured on Jesus at the cross is that he is crucified between two failures – criminals who have committed the serious offence of rebelling against Roman rule. It is a calculated insult on the part of the authorities to say what they think of someone who claims to be a king. The crowd around the cross is mocking and jeering Jesus and, as they do this, one of the criminals joins in. The other rebukes him, saying, 'We are getting what our deeds deserve. But this man has done nothing wrong.'

Then, in an extraordinary statement, he says, 'Jesus, remember me when you come into your kingdom.' It is entirely typical of Christianity's habit of turning things upside down that the first person to acknowledge that the cross was a triumph rather than a disaster was a man at the bottom of society. Those in religious and political authority mock Jesus' kingship; this dying criminal acknowledges it.

In response, Jesus turns to the criminal and makes this wonderful promise. 'Truly I tell you, today you will be with me in paradise.' We see authority in this statement. '*Truly*,' Jesus says. 'You can rely on it because I say it.' What he is saying is not just the sort of wishful hollow words of hope that you hear in hospital wards such as, 'Don't worry, you'll soon be out of here.' It is the most trustworthy of promises.

At the cross, Jesus becomes the ultimate victim, suffering in the place of people. Yet although he loses almost everything on the cross, one thing he retains is his authority. He remains the Lord and as such he is able to make promises. And what a promise it is! 'Truly I tell you, today you will be with me in paradise.' The word 'paradise' means 'a garden' and it is used in the Greek version of the Old Testament for the Garden of Eden. What Jesus is saying is, 'I promise you that *this very day*, you will be in the Garden of Eden with me.' What better words could anyone ever hear? What comfort, what hope, what security are in these words!

We see in this exchange between Jesus and the criminal a picture of the breathtaking and almost incomprehensible nature of God's grace. The criminal on the cross merely acknowledges his own guilt and recognises that Jesus is truly God's king. And this confession is enough for Jesus to accept him and offer him salvation and eternal life.

This doomed, dying man has no opportunity for baptism, good works or charity; all he can do is admit his guilt and affirm that Jesus is Lord. For almost two thousand years men and women in the most terrible and hopeless situations have found in Jesus' promise all the hope they need.

Ponder: *Jesus Christ is the same yesterday, today, and forever.*

Hebrews 13:8, NLT

Prayer: Eternal God, the hope that we have in you is truly staggering. May we live our lives in the light of eternity with you. Amen.

Woman, here is your son . . .
Here is your mother

(John 19:26–27)

THREE

The Gospels tell us that Jesus' mother and a number of the women who had followed him remained by the cross and with them was just one male disciple, 'the disciple whom he loved', traditionally identified as John.

We read that 'When Jesus saw his mother there, and the disciple whom he loved standing near by, he said to his mother, "Woman, here is your son," and to the disciple, "Here is your mother." From that time on, this disciple took her into his home.'

Roman law, with its typical combination of justice and barbarity, allowed that someone who was crucified could, even as they hung on a cross, make a legally binding last will and testament to settle their affairs.

Here, a few hours before his death, Jesus has only one thing left to sort out: his responsibility to his mother. So, as the darkness gathers, he turns to his mother and John and hands her into his care.

It is all too easy to see this as no more than Jesus affirming what we might call 'family values'. We imagine him 'looking after his mum' in the same way as, on the front line, some mortally wounded soldier might ask a comrade to make sure that his family were all right.

Yet carefully thinking about what is going on here points us to something deeper and more radical. For a start we have to ask why Jesus handed his mother into John's care. After all, although it seems likely that by now Joseph had died, the Gospels are clear that Jesus had other biological family. There are several brothers, two of whom become leaders in the early church, and several sisters. Both tradition and culture would suggest that the obvious thing for Jesus to do is to ask John to take his mother back to her family in Nazareth. But he doesn't. He tells John that it is his responsibility to take care of his mother.

What we see here is something that is present throughout the Gospels. Jesus saw his purpose not just to forgive people as individuals but to create through them a new community – a people who would be based not on racial or family ties, but on their relationship to him through faith.

Jesus makes the point that this new community must take priority over the demands of family (Matthew 12:46–49; 13:55–56; Mark 3:35). He is therefore being utterly consistent in entrusting his mother to the care of the community of believers rather than to his relatives.

Here on the cross Jesus looks forward to the coming of the church and demonstrates his faith in its future by committing his mother into its hands.

This is very challenging. Our Western culture emphasises the individual over everything else. Here, Jesus looks away from himself to show both care for family and his commitment to the Christian community. We need to practise this too.

Ponder: *Always be humble and gentle. Be patient with each other, making allowance for each other's faults because of your love.* Ephesians 4:2, NLT

Prayer: Lord, thank you for the reminder that we are part of your family. May we each play our part to encourage our sisters and brothers, so that we can all live our lives to your praise and glory. Amen.

My God, my God,
why have you forsaken me?

(Matthew 27:46 and Mark 15:34)

FOUR

The fourth statement from the cross is both deep and terrible. Mark puts it in its context as follows: 'At noon, darkness came over the whole land until three in the afternoon. And at three in the afternoon Jesus cried out in a loud voice, *"Eloi, Eloi, lema sabachthani?"* (which means, "My God, my God, why have you forsaken me?").' Two things stand out: the intense universal darkness and the cry, so appalling that it was remembered by the first Christians in its original language of Aramaic.

Before we think about how Jesus prays it is worth noticing that, even in this darkest hour, Jesus does pray. Although in agony and in despair, he keeps faith. He was without sin to the last.

Yet it is *how* Jesus prays here that is most striking. As we were reminded in the first statement from the cross, 'Father, forgive . . . ', Jesus normally addressed God with that word of close family trust, 'Abba' or 'Father'. But here, in the midst of a darkness that mirrors his spiritual state, he is reduced to praying with the formal address of 'God'.

Yes, it is a quotation from Psalm 22, but that cannot conceal a real sense of desolation and separation. No human being can understand fully what was going on here. The best interpretation is that Jesus, united with the Father for all eternity, is now experiencing separation from God the Father.

Christians have seen in these appalling words the expression of the great principle of exchange that runs throughout the Gospel. On the cross, for those three hours, Jesus took upon himself our sin, became distanced from God the Father and bore the punishment that should have been ours.

To put it in terms of relationships, Christ's separation as the Son of God allowed our adoption as children of God.

As St Paul writes in 2 Corinthians 5:21, 'God made him who had no sin to be sin for us, so that in him we might become the righteousness of God.'

Jesus went to a place of separation so that we might never need to be separated from God. He cried out these words of abandonment precisely to ensure that his followers should never have to say them.

Ponder: *He personally carried our sins in his body on the cross so that we can be dead to sin and live for what is right. By his wounds you are healed.*

1 Peter 2:24, NLT

Prayer: Dear Jesus, as we read of the agony you went through for us, all we can do is say thank you. Thank you that at the moments we feel isolated and alone you are with us. Help us to reach out to others with your love and compassion. Amen.

I am thirsty

(John 19:28)

FIVE

The fifth saying is brief: 'I am thirsty.' At one level, this is no more than a desperate, agonised cry of suffering. We hear a man on a cross, close to death, suffering from injuries and loss of blood, expressing his need for something to drink.

It is a painful, poignant, utterly human request. In thinking of this we need to be reminded of the truth that, in Jesus, God has suffered with human beings and nowhere more than here at the cross. If we understand and believe the Easter story, however much we may suffer, we can never ever point the finger at God and say, 'You really don't know what this is all about.'

In Christ, God is acquainted with human pain at its most extreme. The God of the universe, the maker of heaven and earth, the one who by a mere word created the very oceans, knew what it was to suffer thirst.

Sooner or later most people find themselves in a place that is deeper, darker and more terrible than they thought possible. At such times the thought that God has been there can be an enormous comfort.

Yet, as with so many sayings in the Gospels, there is another meaning. In John's Gospel Jesus frequently uses the image of water. In chapter 4 he declares that he is the giver of 'living water' to the Samaritan woman, and in John 7:37–38 we read, 'On the last and greatest day of the festival, Jesus stood and said in a loud voice, "Let anyone who is thirsty come to me and drink. Whoever believes in me, as Scripture has said, rivers of living water will flow from within them."'

With this in mind we sense something of the appalling nature of the cross. The maker of all things has become someone who craves a cup of water. Christ became cursed that we might be blessed, became empty so that we might become filled and became nothing that we might become something. That's what the cross is all about.

Ponder: *We know, dear brothers and sisters, that God loves you and has chosen you to be his own people.*

1 Thessalonians 1:4, NLT

Prayer: Lord Jesus, as we see afresh what you went through on the cross for us, may we look beyond our circumstances and see that you are sufficient, that you are the well of water that never runs dry. Amen.

ned

(19:30)

SIX

There's something extraordinarily satisfying about completing something. Whether it's wallpapering the bedroom, writing a report for the office, working out at the gym or just doing the shopping, it's a good moment when we come to the end, breathe a sigh of relief and can say, 'It's finished!'

There is all this – and more – in the sixth word of Christ from the cross. Let's put it in its context. John, in his Gospel, writes, 'Knowing that everything had now been finished, and so that Scripture would be fulfilled, Jesus said, "I am thirsty." A jar of wine vinegar was there, so they soaked a sponge in it, put the sponge on a stalk of the hyssop plant, and lifted it to Jesus' lips. When he had received the drink, Jesus said, "It is finished." With that, he bowed his head and gave up his spirit' (John 19:28–30).

Wrapped up in that little word that we translate as *finished* are ideas of fulfilment, accomplishment and achievement. It is a word not of despair but of triumph, the sort of word that you might gasp out when you cross the finishing line of a marathon.

It is clear that Jesus is not saying '*I* am finished' but rather '*it* is finished'. But what is the *it* that has been finished? In John's Gospel Jesus describes himself several times as someone who has been given work to do by his Father (John 4:34; 17:4). That work, it is clear, is not just calling his disciples or teaching but dying on the cross. To someone familiar with the Jewish faith of Jesus' day what is going on at the cross is almost unsubtle in its obviousness. At this point in the afternoon before the start of Passover, in the temple barely a mile away from the cross, lambs are being sacrificed for the sins of the people of God. Actually what is being 'finished' here is not just Jesus' work, but the whole Old Testament system of practices.

That long and tortuous tale of priests, kings, temples and sacrifices is completed and fulfilled in Christ's death on the cross. In the time before the cross, men and women could only look forward in hope that God would someday find a way to pay off what they had done wrong.

In the time after the cross, men and women look back to this moment with faith and gratitude.

We can actually see in this word 'finished' something very personal. Human religion has often been summarised in the phrase 'the search for salvation'. In every race, culture and age, men and women have struggled to find a way through which they can be right before God. So we find people trying every sort of religious practice – making vows, giving up pleasures, going on pilgrimages and making all manner of sacrifices – in order to try to make themselves right with God.

Here at the cross we see the end of humanity's long quest. If we understand what Jesus did on this cross and trust in him then we can say about our own personal search for salvation, *it is finished*.

Ponder: *Because of Christ and our faith in him, we can now come boldly and confidently into God's presence.*

Ephesians 3:12, NLT

Prayer: Thank you, Lord, that you have wiped our lives clean. May we express our gratitude to you by living our lives in the knowledge of your unconditional love for us. Amen.

Father, into your hands
I commit my spirit

(Luke 23:46)

SEVEN

We read in Luke's Gospel that on the cross Jesus 'called out with a loud voice, "Father, into your hands I commit my spirit." When he had said this, he breathed his last.'

After the physical, psychological and spiritual agony that is shown by most of the seven sayings from the cross this last one blesses us by its difference.

It is a simple, quiet and gentle prayer: 'Father, into your hands I commit my spirit.' In Jewish tradition, these words were used as an evening prayer before going to sleep, so its use here is even more appropriate.

Once more Jesus is quoting a psalm, this time Psalm 31:5 – 'into your hands I commit my spirit' – but has added to it that vital and personal little word 'Father'. The addition of 'Father' to these words is typical of Jesus and the result is a prayer of almost childlike trust and intimacy.

On the cross everything has been battled and fought, but now that appalling storm has blown over. The torment, the agony, the separation – all are now ended. Jesus' work is done and as death creeps over him the darkness that has descended on the world lifts.

The return of that trusting word for God, 'Father', is a quiet confirmation that the appalling, unfathomable gap between Father and Son that existed on the cross is now ended. There is unity once more between Father and Son. Jesus knows that what will be wrapped around him soon are not just grave clothes, but his Father's embrace. There is reunion now and soon there will be resurrection.

We have seen how we can personally identify with many of the words of the cross. We can do this here. This is a good prayer for every difficult and uncertain time in life. If you have come to know God as Father through Christ then it is an appropriate prayer at the start and end of any day, before any danger and before sleep. It is even more appropriate before death. Because of what Jesus did on the cross, whatever we face – even the grave itself – we can commit ourselves securely and confidently into the Father's hands.

Ponder: *Trust in the L*ORD *with all your heart; do not depend on your own understanding.*

Proverbs 3:5, NLT

Prayer: Lord, thank you that whatever we face, today and in the future, we can be confident that you are with us. Help us to go out in this knowledge and to carry your presence to our world. Amen.